D1537119

"You talk when you cease to be at peace with your thoughts"

Khalil Gibran

"As we try to define a poet, Hayaz takes it a step forward—he writes poems and shares his inner most thoughts and feelings.

Professor Vardan Abdo,
Director Parev - TV

*To
Angie
kind Regards*

11/13/21

"NIGHTS OF A NIGHTINGALE"

NAZARET HAYAZ

ILLUSTRATED BY ALBERT ARAKELIAN

ISBN 978-1-63525-968-1 (Paperback)
ISBN 978-1-63525-969-8 (Digital)

Copyright © 2017 by Nazaret Hayaz
All rights reserved. No part of this publication may be reproduced, distributed, or transmitted in any form or by any means, including photocopying, recording, or other electronic or mechanical methods without the prior written permission of the publisher. For permission requests, solicit the publisher via the address below.

Christian Faith Publishing, Inc.
296 Chestnut Street
Meadville, PA 16335
www.christianfaithpublishing.com

This is a work of fiction. Names, characters, places, and incidents either are products of the author's imagination or are used fictitiously. Any resemblance to actual events, locales, or persons, living or dead, is entirely coincidental.

Printed in the United States of America

PUBLISHER'S NOTES

"Be as gentle as you can be;
This is the glory
Grandeur of beauty
Be as gentle as you can be."

"Soulful poetry for the world"

Being a romantic myself, "A Song of A Gentlemen" is undoubtedly my favorite of Nazaret's collection as it depicts romance in its most beautiful form—being kind, being immersed in the very essence of true love. In a world which seems to dilute the healing power of love, this poem outshines, offering a glimpse of hope for the amorous.

As his editor, it has truly been an honor working with Mr. Nazaret Yenikomshuyan in preparing his collection of soulful poetry for the world. Nazaret eloquently presents his heartfelt tales, bringing his inner world to his audience with full sincerity. I believe Nazaret's poetry will touch the hearts of those who come across his fine work deeply, and I look forward to seeing his work be a much deserved success!

Sincerely,
Eleni Theodorou

CONTENTS

THE CLOWN

I am your clown.
This is my crown;
    To give a laugh
    In a world so rough.

I am your clown
I'll give you a smile,
    Even if I drown.
    This is my crown.

I am your clown
If you have no place.
    Please take my bless,
    With my humble grace.

If you are dark and pale,
I shall not bail.
    If you are lost at night,
    I can be your light.

If you see tears,
They are only for me,
    Red, yellow, brown—
    I am your clown.

I always try to give you a smile,
    Even when I cry,
    With my happy eye.

In any storm,
For all I will be warm.
    I am your clown;
    This is my crown.

FOREVER YOUNG

Yesterday I was young,
Yesterday I was drunk.
With my powerful tongue,
I was singing a song.

> I am young today,
> My eyes are bright as rays.
> Let it be that way,
> And don't go away.

When I become old,
Women, I can't hold.
I need not a world of gold;
I am young, not old.

> Tomorrow, tomorrow, tomorrow
> Come back to me, don't go.
> Stay with me like a shadow,
> My young, my young days hello!

Stay, my young days,
Play my childish ways.
Please you stay, stay;
Any day, any day, any day.

AM I GUILTY. OR YOU AND ME?

Before I said good-bye Love,
You flew away like a dove.
Perhaps I am guilty, maybe not.
Your fake passion, still in my blood.

Your restless soul I embrace
Thoughts flood on my face.
      Perhaps I am guilty, maybe not;
      My memories of you, are still hot.

You are my injured bird,
Perhaps I am blameless that you are hurt.
      I will let my soul unite,
      That is made with all light.

YOUR LOVE

From your wild love
Skies dancing high above.
      Your wild kiss,
        I will always miss.

You are my nymph.

      On a sunrise
      Looking in your eyes
      They rise and rise
      To my paradise.

Slow, slowly, slow,
Like immense flow of a rainbow.
      My songs you know,
      To heaven we go.

This was a dream, unseen.

YOUR FALSE SMILE

Thy false smile
Adored for a while.
In my arm
I held your charm.

Thy eye made me fly.
Be it love, be it hate,
I drop the question on your plate.

I gave you my song of light,
That your eyes became bright.
You were always in my sight;
Every day and night…

Perhaps 'twas strong hate
Through your love create.
Like storm one night
You said good night.

WE SEPARATE

Wandering my heart in a haze,
Longing for the sun to blaze.
    Singing fire hopeless,
    I must confess.

Innocent belief of mine
Erasing hopes of a kiss.
    Spirit enters divine,
    With my sense of bliss.

WAKE UP MY LOST YEARS

Wake up, my lost years.
     Inflame my soul
     Like colorful Fall.

Dreams I had seen,
I used to play on the green.
     I was a little boy,
     Oh, what a joy!

My garden of Love,
     Shining stars above,
     Flying like a dove.

Lost pleasures all,
Past treasured all.
     You turned into a ball;
     Gone like flying Fall.

I AM YOUR NEST

I would build my nest
A place for you to rest.
      I will be your sleep,
      That you can rest deep.

I am the echoes of your vein,
I am your fountain.
      Your oasis in the desert,
      I am your nest.

I am your earth.
You fly like a bird
      Anywhere, any night.
      But you return tonight.

LOST LOVE

Deep sleep for many years
Like winter storm madness.
One lost love wakes up old
It cries and said "oh Lord."

Years slid away,
Ambushes enchantment of our day.
Oh moment take my pray,
My hair has become gray.

Dreadful invisible moment wait
You play with my faith.
Oh my lost love, come to me straight;
It's already too late…

NO END

Your wild hair
Dark under, above white
What a delight!

Your legs long,
Straight and strong
Me, to belong!

I am your slave,
If you are brave.
Let's live in a cave.

Holding hands
We roll and bend;
Night shall never end.

HOPE

When women say "no,"
It is better you know.
Instead of hope,
Might you lope.
Until they say "yes,"
Then you impress.

GIVE ME YOUR PASSION

Give me your passion
Filled with emotion.
      Make me fire,
      You to desire!

Give me your passion;
Inflame my soul with your emotion.
      Open your door,
      So I can soar.

Give me your passion,
That in your eye
      I become love of ocean,
      You never cry.

TO ALL WOMEN WHO LIE

When women lie,
They lie and cry.
    I only say hi,
    And pass by.

I smile and smile,
Yet in my eye, they die.
    I will bless
    Those who can say yes.

I will say hello,
Even when they say no.
    Yes or no,
    Ho-ho-ho.

Let them say no;
I will say hello.
    But when they lie,
    I will smile and pass them by.

OH WOMEN

Oh, delightful women,
     Listen to my song;
     It's not long.

Delightful and juicy;
     It's my duty
     To sing to your beauty.

Oh woman, yum-yum!
     Please read the rhyme,
     On time, on time, on time.

Your eyes, bluish-blue;
     Is it you?
     My wish came true.

This is a duet;
     You and your poet!
     Women so delightful,
Don't make me your fool.

On time, on time, on time!
     Oh woman delight,
     You are my light.

ONE DAY AT THE GO-GO BAR

Go-go girls like to hop
They start at bottom, work to top.

They look in your eye
And they say "hi."
If money you have,
Then love you'll had.

I was wondering one day;
My heart liked to play.
Go-go bar it hail,
Love was for sale!

Love was for sale,
"Can I buy?" I hail.
"20 dollars," she said.
"19.99," I said;
"Go to hell," she said.

This is the law,
You know?
You can watch,
But not touch!

She sat on my lap,
Started moving like that.
I am sitting under,
She is moving like thunder.

"Where are you from," I said,
"Brazil is my home," she said.
Oh Brazil, Brazil,
Your women I feel.
Beauties you create,
Your women are great.

WE ARE ESTRANGED

The moment long gone,
Your image only one.
You became a part,
Deep in my heart.

How a moment may
On any given day.
Music my soul played
And I humbly prayed.

How a moment may
Blossom my day;
Not only a day,
But my life, my way.

My life is like a book,
Please open and look.
Any page, any age;
My love I do engage.

OH, MY STARVING LOVE

Oh, my starving Love,
I strive and I strive
       What you need, that I will be
       So that…

Oh, my starving hope,
Vein of love I op.

Life of my journey
Only empire so be.
       My only throne, my own;
       My last hope to be.

Immortal beauty of she
Have I found never yet.
       My last hope yet,
       I never forget.

A SONG OF A GENTLEMAN

Be as gentle as you can be;
This is the glory.
Grandeur of beauty,
Be as gentle as you can be.

Oh be gentle, be it so,
Her feelings for you will grow.
My eyes, my view, always you;
You calm my heart, like morning dew.

I hear her voice, I rejoice
You are only, my only choice.
I live to love,
Be it true love.

My heart throbbing in my chest,
Your smiling face gives me rest.
I am your gentle Gentleman;
Amen, amen, amen.

I play, I pray under oath,
My life to you I devote.
Amen, amen, amen.
I am your only, lonely man.

YOU LIKE TO GO SLOW

Oh I know, I know, I know
Like a flower you grow.
     You like to go slow
     Before I open your flow.

     Like a shadow,
     You, I follow.
     Oh please,
     Don't say "no."

Oh, please don't say "no,"
I like to be your hero.

One night like a sparkling light,
I am like thunder;
You surrender.
I am like thunder;
You, earthquake under.

Oh, please don't say "no,"
I am your hero.
     Like a shadow I follow
     Everywhere you go.

WOMEN AND WINE

One gray day,
Until today
Wine and women,
Compete for men.

Wine said: "Hey mighty men!
                I'll take you to heaven.
                I'll make you cry,
                I'll make you fly!"

Women said: "If not me,
                You'll always be empty;
                I am the fire,
                You are to desire."

Wine said: "Hey, you women,
                Sexually silly;
                If not me,
                Don't you see?
                Your own misery."

Women said: "Hey, you wine,
                You might be fine.
                Don't you see my line?
                Men I play, I dine;
                They are all mine.
                I am delightful
                Men, I fool!"

Author: Fight goes on and on,
Who is…
World of this,
Women or wine?
Unnatural way
We always say.

This is divine
Or
I am fine.
There is no fine line,
In this world of mine.

MY HEART I TRUST

Be it first,
Be it last.
     My heart I trust,
     If my heart lust.

I will always wait,
I will never hate.
     Please don't be late;
     We have a date.

Never too late,
It was so great.
     Relationship deep;
     I shall always keep.

Embracing the moment
With no regret,
     It was enchantment,
     My brunette.

Please don't be late
To our first date.
But even if you are late,
I will never hate.

Be it first,
Be it last,
     Only my heart
     Will I trust.

FOUR LANGUAGES OF LOVE

Everywhere I turn,
Sound to me return.
I go to any hill,
My heart "amore" fill.

     Amore, amore, amore
     All we must have more.

Oh, Armenian "sere"
Oh "em sere, em sere."
Sound of gold we share,
It's beautiful and fair.

     Oh "em sere, em sere."
     Golden sound in the air.

Sound of love English;
Well, Polish distinguish.
When I say "my love,"
You feel all stars above.

     Oh my love, my love
     My hold glove.

Oh Lubove ma-ya,
Russia radnaya ma-ya.
Icy country cold,
Lubove sound gold.

Oh Lubove ma-ya,
Moy gorod moskva.

In any language of love,
Sound flies like a dove.
Let's love each other all,
With peace in everyone's soul.

SPIRIT AND SOUL

Lonely
Only
Spirit
And
Soul.

For all,
For all,
For all.

Spirit and I,
Tell me why?
You thrive,
You strive,
Within my life.

Yet you take my crown
From my head.
My crown, my own;
I hold my breath.

Long I stood
Spirit replies,
Right to my eyes,

It's the mood
You should
You should inspire,
Like a food, your mood desire.

My soul
You are all.
You are my feeling,
You are my living.

Center of my brain,
You come and go like rain.
You are my journey long;
You are my humble song.

My soul, my courage,
You are deep;
Spirit rumbles underneath.
No one recognizes all;
What is a soul?

EGO

Not long ago, I spoke to my Ego.
"Ego," said I, "tell me why?
Is it you that makes me shy?"
He smiled at me and glided by.

"Is it you that I have my pride?
Pride of human, and also of demon.
Come out of me; Don't hide!"
He smiled at me and glided by.

"Is this you that I fight?
You are harping on the same string.
The one and only, I am your king!"
He smiled at me, swinging by.

"Hello, my Ego,
Perhaps you, I now not know."
"Hello, hello," my ego echo.
He smiled at me and silently go.

From centuries and twenty-one,
Time moves on and on.
Our egos a song do sing;
I am your only lonely king.

ONE BEE AND ME

One bee and me.
Bee I like to be.
      Fly free,
      Me and my melody.

Flower to flower,
Nectar I take;
      Honey to make
      Tzz flowers awake.
      Awake flowers, awake.

Bee I like to be,
For you to succeed
And have all you need.

Tzzzzzzzzzz in your ear,
I am singing clear.
      Please come hear,
      Ever so near.

You and I,
Fly so high.
      We fly, fly
      Into the sky.

I will say hi
To each passerby,
      Free from the sky.

SCENE

Mountain chain,
Rainbow and rain.
Raging wind dancing,
Tango with the evening.

Sea breeze and or…
Mountainchain and rain.
Kissing on the shore,
Furrows like veins.

Rain and thunder,
Rumbles earth under.
Whispers through the trees,
The cooling wind breeze.

ME AND THE SEA

Infinite sight
Sea breeze and night.
    Me and the sea,
    Ineffable mystery.

Nothing, nothing, nothing,
Only, sea deep breathing.
    Symphony of sea,
    Only I see.

Foam and sand
Embraced with land.
    Kissing on the shore,
    Love scene and more.

WHO AM I

You and I
We ask ourselves this endless question.
From our revelation,
We go to our imagination.

Often this is our conversation;
Our own blind satisfaction.
We say we are God's creation.

SPRING

Lives ring in Spring,
Dazzling morning.
All grays are gone;
Greens are on.

From womb of earth,
Voices I heard.
Open the land,
Give them your hand.

Ring, ring Spring,
Hopes you bring.
Blossom the trees,
After the freeze.

ENSLAVED BY FAITH

I am enslaved!
Enslaved by faith.
　　Even I believe in lies,
　　With my faithful eyes.

I believe in bad,
I believe and am sad.
　　Even faithfully,
　　I lie to me.

Between you and me,
To find lost truth,
Wherever it could be.

FAITH

Your mysterious, passionate eyes,
My smile takes us to paradise.
Ships of my love takes you to the skies.

No separation on any night,
We rejoice and dance tonight.
Let the faith of happiness light.

Tears of unification overflow,
You wake up and smile like a rainbow.
While my soul is, you know.

Oh, stop and look at me, Miss
Although I am a poet, as you know;
My natural feelings I will follow.

ETERNAL EVENING

Evening wakes up with last rain of drop,
Open the eyes, look to the skies.

Slow and quiet it has been,
Autumn playing violin.

Far, far away, one stream unseen,
Playing music wind to join.

MY UNIVERSE

My universe endless,
With goddesses bless.
Winter or spring,
Heavenly place.

With honest sweat
For women's body;
Blessed as bread.

In my dreams
My hope beams.
Better tomorrow,
Heart always screams.

NOSTALGIA

I close my eye
And memories pass by.
    My mother and I;
    Like eagle, I fly.

My mind like rain,
Crying again.
    If there is a bridge,
    My mother, I reach.

Sweet voice from the sky;
Slow, slowly, slow,
    Said to me "hello,"
    Mellow and hallow.

Sweet voice from the sky
My mother and I;
    Her soul never die,
    In my nostalgic eye.

Dedicated to my mother, a saint, Turvanda.

YOU AND ME

We always say
"You and me";
    But we always think
    "You or me."

It's our ego,
Our minds flow.
    World of gold,
    Only I hold.

Oh, don't you know?
Same paths we go.
    You and me,
    Together we grow…

AMERICA 9-11

Standing proudly,
You embrace all humankind.
With your majesty,
You instill faith in their mind.

Morning was calm and people charmed,
You got assaulted and badly harmed.
We your liberty, raising your arm;
"Nine-eleven," more united we become.

We are the arteries of your heart,
Open to the world a new chart.
May you always fight;
For our human right.

I will always write
That you always fight
For all human right;
You always shine so bright.

You became stronger-stronger,
You live longer and longer.
Your voice flies station to station;
You are a glorious nation!

NEW YORK

Manhattan,   New York
Island of all.
Money street wall;
You gotta walk tall.

Town of China
Oriental stores.
Small-small holes
People look twins;
Oh, what genes.

Little Italy

Street of Mulberry,
Becomes tiny-tinyer;
It's so charming
A world it brings.

Tribecca

New trend!
It's hard to blend.
Old building gone;
New comers come.

O Soho-Soho

Prince and Spring,
Your glory I drink;
Where fashion flow,
One has to come and grow.

Meat Market
> No more!
> Night life we adore;
> Destination of us all.

Chelsea-Chelsea
> Land of gays free.
> You can see any art;
> If desires your heart.

Midtown
> Broadway holds the crown.
> World of show,
> Our mind shall blow.
> Club of Jews;
> It's not news.

Upper West,
> Beautiful and best.
> You have to be rich
> To live and to reach.

Upper East,
> Poor don't exist!
> Windows on Madison;
> Free, you can watch,
> But you can't touch.

Central Park
> If you are pale and dark;
> One should walk and rest,
> Between East and West.

New Harlem,
                Oh, what a shame;
                Whom to blame?
                Youngs moving North,
                Center can't afford.

My New York, New York;
Hi, New York, New York.
You are greatest of all,

"BUSINESSMAN AND THE CLOWN"

Businessman to a clown;
Who is the most honest of all?

Clown, I know for sure,
You are not pure.
  I don't know who,
  That is not you.

TO ALL POLITICIANS

Politicians are creative.
They only believe
How money to make;
From whom to take.

They talk and jumble;
They talk so humble.
          After they rise,
          A promise dries.

EVIL COMES LIKE A SPARK

Evil comes like a spark,
Makes our mind dark
    If we are to be kind,
      We must leave behind.

EVERY DAY IS A GOOD DAY

Every day is a good day.
Let it rain, let it rain.
I will sing again.

It's beautiful, hey-hey,
This morning, today.
     Sunshine afternoon,
     And evening, full moon.

Every day is a good day.
Don't you see? Hey, hey.
     With nature I play—
     I play my way.

Night is dark,
My heart a spark.
     It brings you light,
     A future always bright.

EVERLASTING PEACE

Let it storm,
Anywhere from.
     A tempest be born;
     I will play my horn.

Let it rain tonight,
Up until the morning light.
     New lives to be born,
     All I play is my horn.

I will play my horn,
Melody of peace;
     Everyone to please.
     My notes, piece by piece.

We say "no to war!"
We say "no to war!"
     Love grows more and more.
     Fly from door to door.

My music on the highest note
Comes to the end.
     We all hand in hand;
     We have to blend.

We must share and care;
We are a band,
In God's holy land.

THE POET'S RENAISSANCE

Cornerstone of literature
Crystal vision of the future.
You, William Shakespeare,
With your "King Lear,"
With your "Hamlet" noble
Your bright thought, global.
Open the face
With your charming grace;
No one can replace.

Oh Lord, Oh Lord, Oh
Edgar Allen Poe.
You hold the throne,
"Tamarlane" your own.

Your sound of "Bell"
Flies heaven to hell.
The way you define the tone
Takes your literary pantheon.

"In the icy air of night,
With crysaline delight."

And you, Byronyan Lord,
Estranged universe you behold.
And this that you wrote,

For a man to become a poet,
He must be in love, or miserable.

Nazaret reciting Poems at Armenian Radio Hour of New Jersey

Nazaret with his wife Gohar

Poet Antranik Marashyan
(Nazaret's brother)

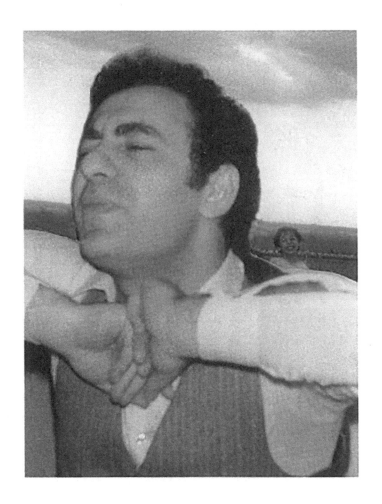

Printed in U.S.A.
Copyright © 2016

ABOUT THE AUTHOR

Nazaret Hayaz was born in the small village of Vanashen in Armenia that overlooked the Mount Ararat where according to the biblical story Noah's Ark landed.

Most likely, Nazaret, at an early age, was enraptured by the majesty of Ararat. In the view of Ararat, Nazaret felt contentment and pride, which made him compose poems alongside his brother Antranig.

In 1980, Nazaret and his entire family moved to The United States where among the Armenian Community, he actively participated in the cultural and theatrical performances. After his affiliation with Armenian radio, Nazaret recited Western and Eastern Classical poetry on the air. He currently resides in River Edge, New Jersey with his family and continues to write.

Poetry is my life. I started writing poetry at the age of thirteen. At school, I was always reciting poetry, and my teacher of literature liked it very much. At that time, my older brother, Antranik Marashian was an accomplished poet, and I admired his philosophy. I had read many poets; however, none of them inspired me. My inspiration has been nature. Nature has always been an enigma for me. I'm trying to discover the secrets of nature and relate them true to the world. I am trying to discover the secrets of nature and relate them true to the world. I am trying to discover the characteristics between men and women, and I believe I have accomplished that.

After high school, I studied at the Armenian Veterinarian University between 1975 and 1979. In 1979, I immigrated to the

United States of America with my family. Most of the time, I write at night. It is fantastic being with yourself and talking to your inner world. Often, you find something new in you. If you do this, you will never get bored and life becomes more and more beautiful and interesting.

CPSIA information can be obtained
at www.ICGtesting.com
Printed in the USA
LVHW051023280121
677352LV00005B/129

9 781635 259681